PARASAIL

Prirodoslovni muzej Dubrovnik

LEONE
trattoria LEONE trattoria
Renaissance Garden

EXCURSIONS

EXCURSIONS
EXCHANGE
ACCOMMODATION

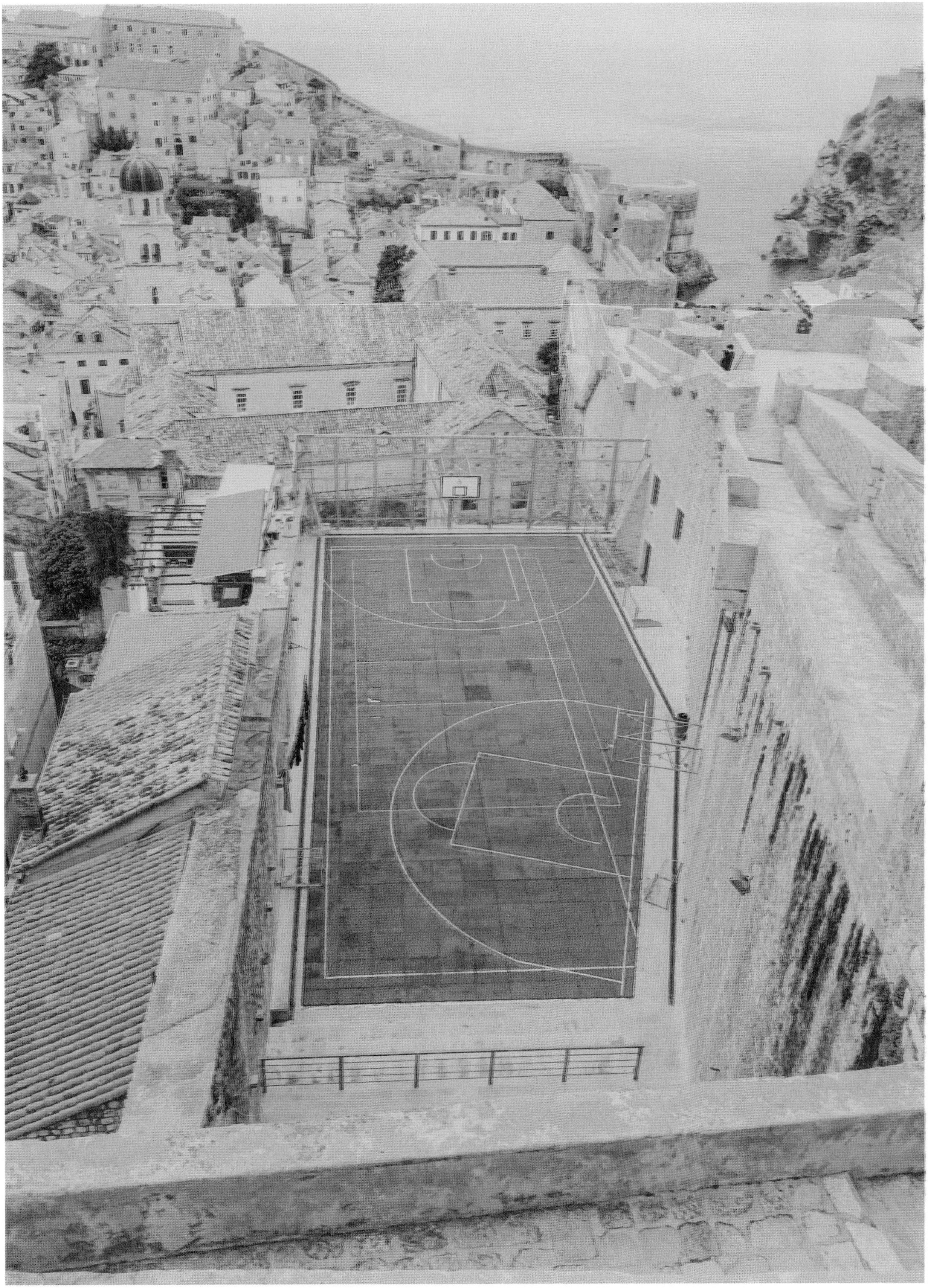

POKLISAR
restaurant
terrace
pizzeria
caffe
breakfast
toilet

Printed in Great Britain
by Amazon

23840248R00025